FINDING MESSI

The Miracle Cat From Kyiv

Trevor
Ostfeld

Iryna
Chernyak

Illustrated by
Katherine
Blackmore

GREENLEAF
BOOK GROUP PRESS

This book is a reflection of the author's present recollections of experiences over time. Its story and its words are the author's alone. Some details and characteristics may be changed, some events may be compressed, and some dialogue may be recreated.

Published by Greenleaf Book Group Press
Austin, TX
www.gbgpress.com

Distributed by Greenleaf Book Group

For ordering information or special discounts for bulk purchases, please contact Greenleaf Book Group at PO Box 91869, Austin, TX 78709, 512.891.6100.

Design and composition by Greenleaf Book Group
Cover design by Greenleaf Book Group and Katherine Blackmore
Illustrations by Katherine Blackmore

Publisher's Cataloging-in-Publication data is available.

Print ISBN: 979-8-88645-178-8
eBook ISBN: 979-8-88645-179-5

Manufactured through APO on acid-free paper
Manufactured in China on 1/16/24

24 25 26 27 28 29 30   10 9 8 7 6 5 4 3 2 1

First Edition

AUTHORS' NOTE

This book is based on a true story.

Between February and March of 2022, more than half of the children of Ukraine left their homes to escape violence following the Russian invasion. Millions of people crossed the border from Ukraine to Poland, almost all of whom were women and children.

Iryna Chernyak and her mother Alexandra are two of those people.

To the children
of Ukraine

Have you ever
met a cat
that plays soccer?

Introducing—Messi, the dribbling,
passing, goal-scoring cat!

My family adopted Messi when
I was eight years old.

I named her after my
favorite soccer player, Lionel Messi.

He just won the World Cup!

Messi was always an inside cat,
so she stayed home when I went
to school and to dance class.

She liked to sit on our couch and look
out the window over the city of Kyiv.

When my mom got home from work
and I got home from school,
Messi would jump off the couch.

Time for
soccer practice!

As Messi got bigger, she got better at chasing
little soccer balls all over our apartment.

And as I got bigger, I got better at finding them.

Between the couch cushions.

Under my bed.

Inside my duffel bag.

Can you find the soccer balls?

Every night, my mom would tuck both of us into bed.

"Good night, Iryna,"
she said to me.

"Good night, Messi,"
she said to the cat.

"Good night, Mama,"
I answered.

I dreamed about dancing.
Messi dreamed about soccer.

And every morning when I woke up,
my *kishka*—that's Ukrainian for "cat"—
was snuggled up beside me.

One Friday night, I threw one of Messi's soccer balls too close to the Shabbat candles.

Mama was surprised and not very happy.

Messi hid behind the couch.

The winter after I turned 11,
Messi and I played a new game.

I had a dance competition coming up,
and I needed an audience.

Turn, jump, kick. Turn, jump, kick!

Messi waited patiently for me to finish
my routine so I could start throwing
her soccer balls again.

As my dance competition got closer,
Mama started getting a lot of phone calls.

She was always listening to the news.
She stopped watching me practice.

But Messi still watched.

Four days before my dance competition,
Mama said we had to leave our apartment.

I could only pack what I could fit into one suitcase.

I cried.

I didn't want to miss my
dance competition!

"Don't worry," Mama said. "We won't be gone long. But we can't stay here in Kyiv. We need to drive away from the fighting and the loud noises."

"Maybe we will be back in time for the competition," I said hopefully.

"But what about Messi?" I asked.

"Messi is an inside cat," Mama reminded me.
"We will leave her food out, and Grandpa will come by to
check on her every morning. We will be back in a few days."

I cried again.

If there were going to be fighting and loud noises,
I wanted my *kishka* with me.

The next morning,
I did not go to school.
Mama did not go to work.

I gave Messi a big hug.

I hid soccer balls for her all over the apartment
so she could play while we were away.

"I will be home soon, my *kishka*," I whispered.

It seemed like all of my friends
were leaving home.

Mama and I drove in traffic
to a new city called Lviv.

"It will just be for a few days,"
Mama said.

But it was not just a few days.

Mama called Grandpa at home in Kyiv.

"Everyone is worried," he told her. "There are loud bangs and shrieking sirens."

Grandpa said he had to stay home to be safe.

Just like Messi, our inside cat.

Mama needed to find someone to check on Messi.

A man we met in Lviv was going back to Kyiv!

Mama gave him the keys to our apartment,
and I told him all about my *kishka*.

But when the man returned to
Kyiv, danger was everywhere.

Explosions.

People fighting.

Wailing sirens.

He had to stay inside too.

Who will help Messi?

Mama called a taxi company, and a brave driver said he would go inside our apartment to take care of my *kishka*.

Have you ever heard of a cat taking a taxi by herself?
That's what Messi did.

The taxi driver went to our apartment to pick up Messi
and then drove her to our friend's house.

I hoped she wasn't scared.

Our friend sent pictures of Messi and said
she would drive her to Mama and me in Lviv.

Lviv—that's where we were the day I was supposed to
have my dance competition and the day
I was supposed to go back to school.

We waited with all the other families
to decide what to do next.

I waited for my *kishka*.

A few days later, Mama said to me, "People are still fighting, and it isn't safe here either.

We need to go to Poland. We cannot stay in Ukraine. We need to leave Lviv."

"What about Messi?" I cried.

"How will she find us in Poland?"

I was scared as we packed to move even farther away from my *kishka*.

The next day, we got more bad news.

Our friend brought Messi to Lviv—where she ran out the door and was lost!

Mama and I posted photos of Messi online.

Many people wrote back, "Is this your cat?"

No.

"Is this your cat?"

No.

"Is this—"

No.

Three weeks went by.

Every day, Mama and I checked our
messages online and posted about Messi.

Every day, Mama's phone was full of news
about people fighting—and about
people like us, far from home.

Some mornings, I woke up and
looked around our plain hotel room.

I looked out the window at this
new city, and I forgot why I was there.

I forgot why Messi wasn't next to me.

But then I remembered.

One day, a woman from Lviv
sent us a photo—"Is this Messi?"

Yes!

It was her.

And more good news—my stepdad
was coming from Lviv to
Warsaw the next day.

That morning, I was so excited;
I woke up before Mama.

My stepdad called and said
he was at the hotel.

Mama and I raced downstairs.

I ran across the lobby to my *kishka*!

Messi was finally home with me.

Well, not exactly home.

I don't know when we will be back in Kyiv.

But for now, home is where we are together.

ACKNOWLEDGMENTS

First and foremost, thank you to Iryna and Alexandra Chernyak for sharing your story and inspiring me. Thank you to Katherine Blackmore for bringing this narrative to life with your vibrant illustrations. Thank you to Rabbi David-Seth Kirshner for leading our group to Poland and Ukraine and for giving me an opportunity to help. Thank you, Jonathan Ornstein with the JCC Krakow and the staff at the Jewish Agency for Israel for your continued work in supporting families seeking refuge from the war in Ukraine. Thank you to Anastasiya Shevchenko for translating and for your valuable perspective. Thank you, Greenleaf Book Group and my editors for helping me share this story with readers around the world. Thank you, Mom, Dad, Vivian, and Evelyn.

—Trevor

I am grateful to everyone who helped save my pet! Thank you to the taxi driver who was not afraid to take Messi from our house in Kyiv when the war started. Thanks to my grandfather who sheltered her. Thank you to the kind woman who found our Messi after she was lost in Lviv. Thanks to my stepdad, Zohar, who brought her to Warsaw. And thank you to my Mama who helped me tell this story. I'm so glad that we met such kind people as Jen, Scott, and Trevor Ostfeld. Thanks to Trevor for sharing my story and for caring about children in Ukraine.

—Iryna

ABOUT THE AUTHORS

Trevor Ostfeld is a seventeen-year-old high school junior in New York City. In March of 2022, three weeks after Russia invaded Ukraine, Trevor and his dad traveled to Poland and Ukraine to deliver humanitarian supplies and to offer support for people displaced by the war. Their group from Temple Emanu-El in Closter, New Jersey met Iryna and Alexandra Chernyak in Warsaw. Trevor hopes that sharing Iryna's story will help people understand the impact of war on families and young children.

Trevor lives in New Jersey with his parents, his two younger sisters, Vivian and Evelyn, and his dog, Rocket.

Iryna Chernyak is a thirteen-year-old seventh class student in Warsaw, Poland. Until late February 2022, Iryna lived with her mom, Alexandra, in Kyiv, Ukraine. She enjoys contemporary dance and playing the guitar. Iryna hopes that her story gives people hope, that even when times are tough, you should never give up.

Iryna lives in Warsaw with her mom, stepdad, baby sister, Mia, and her cat, Messi.

Iryna and Messi reunited, March 2022